The Wonderful World of Coca-Cola

Trade-mark ®

by **MARTIN SHARTAR** and **NORMAN SHAVIN**
designed by KATHLEEN OLDENBURG KING editorial supervisor: Bruce Galphin

CONTENTS

"The Wonderful World of Coca-Cola" is Copyright 1978 by the Publisher, Perry Communications, Inc., 2181 Sylvan Road, SW, Atlanta, Georgia 30344.

Printer: Perry Communications, Inc.

"Coca-Cola," "Coke" and the shape of the contoured Coca-Cola Bottle are registered trademarks of The Coca-Cola Company. The illustrations in this book are all the property of The Coca-Cola Company and are used by its permission and with the cooperation of The Coca-Cola Company Archives of Atlanta, Georgia.

With the exception of the rights to the usage of the illustrations, which belong to The Coca-Cola Company, all rights to "The Wonderful World of Coca-Cola" are reserved, including the rights of reproduction and in any form or by any means, including the making of copies by any photo process, or by any mechanical or electronic device, printed or written or oral, or recording for sound or visual reproduction or for use in any knowledge or retrieval system or device, unless permission in writing is obtained beforehand from the publisher or its authorized representative.

In addition to those persons credited above, this book was made possible through the cooperation of Philip Mooney, The Coca-Cola Company's archivist, and Harold Terhune, photographer. Research for factual and illustrative material was turned from chore to refreshing pause by their courtesy, the assistance of William Pruett and Joseph Wilkinson of The Coca-Cola Company, and the courtesy of staff members of The Coca-Cola Company Archives, Barbara Moore, Karin Giroux and Janet Pecha.

"The Wonderful World of Coca-Cola" was conceived and supervised by the Special Projects Division of Perry Communications, Inc.

*International Standard Book Number 0-933238-01-0.
Library of Congress Catalogue Card No. 78-71521
First Edition/First Printing: December, 1978
Second Edition/First Printing: April, 1979*

The Taste of America:

In a single sip connoisseurs of Coca-Cola can tell what size container it came from and how long it was chilled before being poured over ice. Serve them an arctic-cold Coke in the classic 6½-ounce bottle and watch nostalgia glaze their eyes as memories of earlier encounters with the bubbly brew sparkle into view.

Some can remember their first taste, all mixed up with the flavors and aromas of childhood summers, of picnics, backyard barbecues, baseball games. Or the way Coke eased a fumbling first date in high school at a soda fountain booth as far as possible from staring, giggling classmates. Or the way it tasted to a battle-weary GI during World War II after he'd gone without a Coke for weeks or months. Or the most recent occasion when things went better with Coke—your choice of things. Or when Coke last added life to whatever life you lead.

Fanciers of the tawny beverage are uncountable. If U.S. consumers drank only half of the total daily worldwide production, the entire population would enjoy at least one serving of Coke a day.

As almost everybody knows, whether steady consumer or sometime sipper, there's a secret to Coca-Cola. It's been labeled "7X," but only a handful of executives know its identity. It's a secret so well kept that those who've tried to analyze the contents of Coke settle for calling it "A really *secret* secret."

Coca-Cola's ads are a document of America's changing styles and lifestyles. The calendar girl for 1898 wears fashionably bouffant mutton-chop sleeves and, like her contemporaries, has left her Victorian bustle somewhere behind her.

Leaving the Sixties, a mini-skirted miss and her long-locked companion contemplate the real thing in a world of escalating change.

Turn-of-the-Century opera star Lillian Nordica appeared in early ads for Coca-Cola on posters, calendars, serving trays and change trays. She was best known for her portrayal of Wagner's heroines—the three Brunnhildes, Isolde, Elsa. In 1913 Nordica embarked on what was to have been a farewell world tour, but her ship wrecked in the Malay archipelago. She was taken to Java and died there.

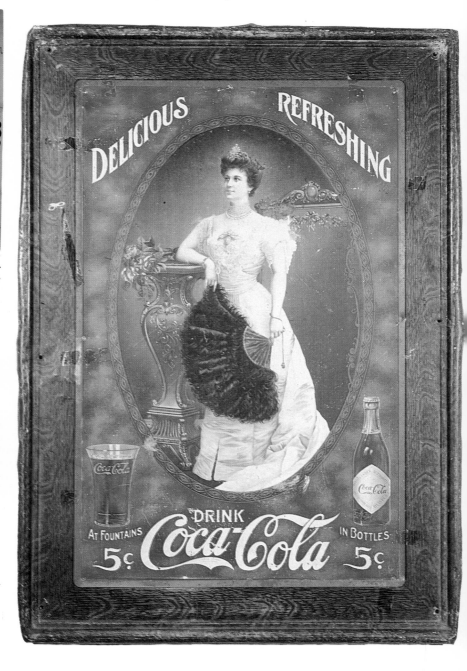

Secret and Familiar

But the really *secret* secret of Coke is familiarity. From the beginning in a kettle in a downtown Atlanta backyard in 1886, makers of Coca-Cola have insisted that wherever it's brewed, a Coca-Cola must taste like a Coca-Cola and nothing else. And since nothing else tastes like a Coke, its preparation never deviates from carefully guarded formulas.

The richest formula of Coca-Cola can be distilled from the stuff of history, from the changing times that Coke was born into and grew with. Times as different as the worlds of opera star Lillian Nordica and movie queen Racquel Welch; changes as vast as the difference between horse-and buggy America and a world whose limits have soared into outer space.

What lies between is mirrored in the world of advertisements for Coca-Cola showing the shift from corseted ladies barely out of bustles to Flappers flirting with new-found freedoms to their free-swinging descendants striding into the Seventies.

Going back to the origin of Coca-Cola is to journey through time to a world whose newest marvels were indoor plumbing and the just-perfected telephone and the incandescent lamp. A list of the alterations in culture and technology that followed sketches the profile of the 20th Century and charts its changing decades.

From the beginning, Coca-Cola was there to give flavor to the years. To return to that beginning, imagine the flavor of the latest dance craze—the waltz—or the sound of a new ballad, "Mother Was A Lady," or the feel of Southern heat on a humid May afternoon before air conditioning could cool men in starched collars and Edwardian jackets or women corseted and pinched at the waist, shrouded from chin to toe in yards of cloth.

Refresh yourself
DRINK
Coca-Cola
Delicious and Refreshing

This 1925 ad shows decades of change and high fashion from the mid-Twenties. Bobbed hair, sleeveless shirtwaists and shorter skirts were emblems of growing freedom from past restraints. The popular turban was often knotted, with scarf trailing along one shoulder, but here the foxtail stole dominates neck and shoulders.

For 1971 The Coca-Cola Company offered a tribute to things unique and uniquely American: a moon-shot view of earth, the Grand Canyon, the American Beauty Rose, Empire State Building, Bald Eagle and Niagara Falls. Young woman borrows 50-year-old hair style.

What's in a Coke?

Fortune magazine once claimed that Coca-Cola is 99 per cent sugar and water. One taste will tell they're there, but it's the other 1 per cent that counts, and few of the most devoted patrons of Coca-Cola can tell what that's made from.

A chemist once identified the ingredients of Coca-Cola — called "merchandises" — for E. J. Kahn Jr.'s *The Big Drink*, an unofficial history of the great quencher: caramel, caffeine, phosphoric acid, and a blend of three parts coca and one part cola. (Coca and cola don't even head the list; they're "Merchandise No. 5.")

Other chemists have identified such kitchen-pantry spices as cinnamon and nutmeg. There's vanilla and vegetable-based glycerin (since that's not derived from pork, Coke is acceptable as kosher to Orthodox Jews and also acceptable to Orthodox Moslems), lime juice and citrus oils, lavender and guarana (extracted from seeds of a Brazilian shrub).

Finally, there's 7X, which Kahn calls "a really secret secret ingredient."

Even if you could find a batch of 7X and added the drink's not-so-secret ingredients, chances of brewing anything that would be recognized as Coca-Cola are far slimmer than the neck of its bottle. The real thing is measured, mixed and bottled according to standards so strict they govern even the purity and taste of the water used in Coke.

What's more, the trademark is as closely guarded as the formula, and what would you do with bootleg Coke if you could copy it? As early as 1927, ads for Coca-Cola boasted "Around the Corner from Anywhere," and that now means 135 countries whose inhabitants take refreshing pauses to the measure of more than 200 million bottles every day.

Enter the Prime-Time Players

John Styth Pemberton created it. Frank M. Robinson named it and gave it a signature. Asa Griggs Candler bought it and made Coca-Cola one of the world's most famous trademarks and its best-known taste.

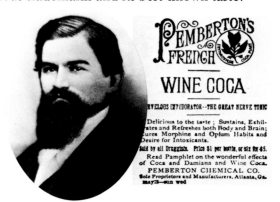

PEMBERTON? There was no question mark in 1886 when *The Atlanta Constitution* described him: "Who of Atlanta's citizens does not recognize the pleasant, benign face, the patriarchal beard and kindly eyes of our well-known and universally respected fellow-townsman, Dr. J. S. Pemberton?" (The title was honorary; he was a pharmacist, not a medical doctor.)

The newspaper's article concluded: "In 1879 Dr. Pemberton, having achieved a competency, retired from wholesaling drugs and embarked in the business of manufacturing proprietary medicines. In this he has met with varying success, and is now on the high road to fortune, with his immense manufactory of Pemberton's Wine-Coca."

A month later, the wine gave way to other flavors, including extract of cola, and Atlanta's four soda fountains were advertising and selling a new drink called Coca-Cola for five cents a glass.

Advertising—at Pemberton's expense—outstripped sales. The first year's figures: $73.96 for advertising and not quite $50 in sales. Pemberton had learned the power of advertising while promoting Indian Queen Hair Dye and such remedies as Globe Flower Cough Syrup, Triplex Liver Pills, Gingerine and Extract of Styllinger.

Pemberton's French Wine-Coca was, he said, a "Marvelous Invigorator—The Great Nerve Tonic. Delicious to the taste; Sustains, Exhilarates and Refreshes both Body and Brain."

His first ad for Coca-Cola proclaimed "Delicious! Refreshing! Exhilarating! Invigorating! The New and Popular Soda Fountain Drink, containing the properties of the wonderful coca plant and the famous cola nuts."

New it was, but to make it popular Pemberton decorated storefronts and soda fountains with oilcloth banners, used streetcar signs and newspaper ads, printed thousands of free-sample coupons, all introducing Coca-Cola as Atlanta's newest taste sensation.

They succeeded, but a year later Pemberton was running out of funds. He sold two-thirds interest in Coca-Cola, starting a financial dance as new owners changed partners who then changed again. Pemberton even added a twist, selling an interest in his remaining share. But they were like dancers stumbling at the start of Pemberton's high road to fortune.

In August, 1888, Pemberton died. Among the poor man's pallbearers was a young Atlanta druggist who had invested in Coca-Cola four months earlier. By April 22, 1891, he was its sole owner.

ASA GRIGGS CANDLER apprenticed himself at 19 to a Cartersville, Ga., pharmacist, reading medical books at night before going to sleep on a cot in the pharmacy's back room.

Clockwise from above left: Coca-Cola was created in the back yard of this Atlanta house, near the present-day Omni International complex. The Asa G. Candler Co., 47 Peachtree Street, was The Coca-Cola Company's home 1888-91. Coca-Cola was first served at Jacob's Pharmacy, which housed operations during 1887. The Coca-Cola Company moved to upper stories of this Decatur Street building in 1891. New York Clothing Company complained syrup sometimes leaked downstairs.

Three years later, in 1873, Candler headed for Atlanta. It was already Georgia's capital, a boom town with a population rising past 21,000.

With $1.50 in his pocket, Candler toured the town's drugstores, seeking work. Early in the day, he applied at J. S. Pemberton's firm; by nine o'clock he was working—on approval, with no salary—at George J. Howard's pharmacy, ending his first day at midnight.

Even a bare outline of Candler's life lives up to its Horatio Alger prologue. *1877:* Candler becomes partner in Hallman and Candler, Wholesale and Retail Druggists. *1878:* Marries former employer's daughter; Howard disapproves, but is reconciled by year's end. *1882:* Enters partnership with father-in-law as Howard & Candler. *1883:* Their building burns; Howard and Candler buy the drug firm of Pemberton, Iverson & Denison. Pemberton founds a chemical company. *1886:* Candler buys out Howard, renames firm Asa G. Candler & Company. Pemberton creates Coca-Cola. *1888:* Candler purchases the shares sold by Pemberton the year before. *1891:* Coca-Cola belongs to Candler.

The punch line is better than Horatio Alger's best: Candler pays $2,300 for Coca-Cola. In 1917, Candler retires as president of The Coca-Cola Company, gives 99 per cent of his stock to family members as a Christmas gift after being elected Mayor of Atlanta. In 1919, without consulting him, Candler's family sells The Coca-Cola Company for $25 million.

FRANK M. ROBINSON, Pemberton Chemical Company's bookkeeper, is credited with naming Coca-Cola and designing its familiar flowing script. He thought "the two C's would look very well in an advertisement," he said later.

Miffed when Pemberton sold off the stock as personal rather than Company property (Robinson had been a partner in the chemical firm), Robinson soon joined Asa G. Candler & Company as bookkeeper and traveling representative. Candler was promoting DE-LEC-TA-LAVE—"for cleansing and preserving the teeth and perfuming the breath."

He told the first convention of bottlers of Coca-Cola in 1909 that Robinson generated the excitement about Coca-Cola, adding "I saw nothing behind it to make anybody want to buy it." But as advertising director until his retirement in 1916, Robinson urged millions to *want* to buy it.

Pemberton's Paraphernalia

The creator of Coca-Cola sold a two-thirds interest in his product to George S. Lowndes, an Atlanta businessman, and Willis Venable, who had served the first Coca-Cola at Jacobs' Pharmacy. Included in the sale was Pemberton's inventory of ingredients, equipment and advertising supplies: Total value, $283.29.

How Candler Did It

"Sometimes a man awakens to find that he owns more of a venture than he intended to, and that's how I became owner of Coca-Cola. There were two young fellows always mixing things up in our town. I was a small town druggist and my store was a clubhouse for a lot of the boys. I trusted them all. Had to, in fact.

"Those boys had a soda fountain mixture and when I began to foot up my ledger, I found that I had more invested in the scheme than the boys. I took it over.

"It didn't take particularly well. It was work to get it started and more work to keep it going."

Asa Candler
1921 interview/*Kansas City Times*

In the Beginning . . .

1886—J. S. Pemberton creates Coca-Cola.

The Statue of Liberty is dedicated. A Centennial gift from the people of France to America, Liberty's arm and torch had been displayed at the 1876 Philadelphia Exposition.

Robert Louis Stevenson publishes *Dr. Jekyll and Mr. Hyde;* Arthur Conan Doyle introduces Sherlock Holmes.

President Grover Cleveland, age 49, marries Miss Frances Folsom in a White House ceremony. She was half his age and less than half his size. Cleveland's favorite joke at the expense of his girth was the story that he was Washington's most polite gentleman. When he offered a lady his seat, three could sit down.

1888—George Eastman perfects box camera and roll film.

1889—Thomas Edison, with Eastman, develops first movie film.

1891—Edison patents movie camera and radio.

1892—First gas- and electric-powered autos manufactured in United States.

The Soda Fountain of Youth

It was an age of folk-cures and over-the-counter nostrums—and little wonder. Think of pain in a time when doctors were few and medicine was primitive.

Try to imagine a headache in a world before aspirin. Until its invention in 1899 (it was first marketed in Germany in 1905), headache cures ranged from "soak the feet in hot water for 15 minutes, drink some warm herb tea, retire to bed, and take a good sweat for about an hour" to "drink 2 tea-spoonfuls of finely powdered charcoal dissolved in half a tumbler of water."

For severe attacks, sufferers were urged to try an application of "Good Samaritan," made of alcohol, oils of sassafras, hemlock, spirits of turpentine, balsam of fir, chloroform, tincture of catechu and guaiacum, oil of origanum, oil of wintergreen and gum camphor.

It was made in two-quart batches, and any of the "noble liniment" left over could be used for rheumatism, bruises, neuralgia, sprains, burns and spinal affections.

It was easier to head for a spa, built near the site of mineral springs—Nature's own bubbly, and the bubblier the better. Soda fountains took the spring out of the spa and brought it into town; since fountains were in drug stores, they lured city-dwellers in need of cures. Within a few decades they'd concentrate on curing thirst.

Even Asa Candler, whose chronic headaches had introduced him to Coca-Cola, would emphasize refreshment *and* relief.

AFTER THE THEATRE
DRINK A GLASS OF Coca-Cola 5¢

It relieves fatigue and excitement, and induces a spirit of thorough, restful satisfaction as delightful to the senses as Coca-Cola is to the sense of taste.

CHICKEN SANDWICH	20		ICE COLD COCA-COLA	5
HAM & CHEESE SANDWICH	25		COFFEE OR TEA	5
HOT ROAST BEEF	35		APPLE PIE	10
FRIED CHICKEN	40		CHERRY PIE	10

DRINK Coca-Cola

Neighborhood Club... Admission 5¢

The Flavor of the Times

Venable's Soda Fountain, situated at what is now downtown Atlanta's Five Points, called itself "The King of All Fountains" with "all the noted reliable health giving mineral waters of the country on draught." In June, 1886, Venable's newspaper ads boasted:

"Why spend so much money to go to the springs to get the benefit of the water, when you can buy it right at home?

"The rapidly increasing Salt spring water is excellent for the kidneys, for dyspepsia, the general system and various disorders.

"Tate springs are of world-wide reputation for the liver, kidneys, digestive organs, a laxative and tonic for the system.

"Glenn springs and Rhea springs are splendid for chronic diarrhea or dyspepsia.

"Saratoga High Rock; Saratoga Excelsior; Vichy; Seltzer.

"These waters are delightful beverages, are laxative in effect, and act splendidly upon the system.

"Kentucky Blue Lick, known everywhere as a splendid appetizer, and to build up the general system.

"Blue Ridge Springs, celebrated everywhere for dyspepsia.

"Buffalo Lithia; Farmville Lithia."

At the end of his ad, Venable listed 35 soda flavors. Among them were Sarsparilla, Orget and Milk Shake — "all the rage." And John S. Pemberton's new flavor, available only in Atlanta, which the ad identified as "Coco-cola."

Do-It-Yourself Receipts

For 19th Century Americans remote from mineral springs, health spas *and* city soda fountains, there were recipes for home-made flavorings. "Dick's Encyclopedia of Practical Receipts & Processes" offered 49 varieties selected from the "Druggist's Circular and Chemical Gazette."

First step: **Simple Syrup.** To 8 pounds finest white sugar, add 2 quarts water and the whites of 2 eggs; stir until all the sugar is dissolved; simmer for 2 or 3 minutes; skim well, and strain through a fine, flannel bag.

With **Simple Syrup** as a base, at-home fountaineers could concoct such delights as these:

Lemon Syrup: Add to simple syrup, when cold, 20 drops fresh oil of lemon and ½ ounce citric acid (previously dissolved in 3 ounces water) to each gallon. Mix by shaking well in a bottle, then add 4 ounces gum solution, made by dissolving 2 ounces fine white gum-arabic in 2 ounces warm water.

Sarsaparilla Syrup: Take oil of wintergreen, 10 drops; oil of anise, 10 drops; oil of sassafras, 10 drops; fluid extact of sarsaparilla, 2 ounces; simple syrup, 5 pints; powdered extract of liquorice, ½ ounce; mix well.

Orgeat Syrup. Take 3 ounces sweet almonds and ½ ounce bitter almonds; gum-arabic in powder, ½ ounce; sugar in powder, 3 ounces. Rub together in a mortar, adding water from time to time, until the mixture measures 1 quart. Strain through a cloth, and mix with 1 gallon of **Simple Syrup.**

End of an Era

Despite the nickname, the "Gay Nineties" were sometimes grim. Politicians and economists argued the merits of silver and gold. The U. S. Census counted some 62 million Americans, one-third of whom lived in urban areas. The Indian Wars were ended; there was no more unsettled frontier.

"How The Other Half Lives," Jacob Riis' grim 1890 report on urban poverty, added a phrase to the language. Child labor increased in the Southern states, still recovering from Reconstruction. The Sherman Anti-Trust Act was passed by Congress, reflecting estimates that 1 per cent of the U.S. population possessed more wealth than the other 99 per cent.

There was a global influenza epidemic in 1890. Widespread famine in Russia in 1891 and in India in 1897.

The world's economy was plunged into a severe Depression in 1893, but the Alaskan gold rush of 1897 boosted U.S. hopes. The war with Spain, "a splendid little war," gave patriotism a lift—and made the United States an international power.

Coca-Cola — DELICIOUS REFRESHING 5¢

IT IS A BEVERAGE IN WHICH A TOAST TO HEALTH AND HAPPINESS BECOMES AN ACCOMPLISHED FACT, AS WELL AS A DELIGHTFUL PLEASURE. AT ALL FOUNTS AND IN BOTTLES

This card entitles you to one glass of Coca-Cola FREE. Present this at fountain of

Decade of Change

Many events and discoveries that brought the 19th Century to a close would determine the shape of the century to come.

1890—First steel-framed building erected in Chicago.

1892—Diesel patents internal combustion engine.

1893—Hawaii is declared a republic; Henry Ford builds his first car.

1894—J. P. Morgan organizes Southern Railroad Company.

1895—Roentgen discovers x-rays; Marconi invents wireless telegraphy; Lumiere brothers invent motion-picture camera.

1896—Hydroelectric plant opens at Niagara Falls; A. H. Becquerel discovers radioactivity; first public motion pictures shown in New York.

1897—Gold stampede begins in the Klondike.

1898—Spanish-American War begins; Pierre and Marie Curie discover radium and polonium; M. J. Owens invents bottle-making machine; first photographs taken using artificial light.

1899—Pres. McKinley signs peace treaty with Spain; 50 U.S. firms produce self-propelled vehicles in large numbers. (They include electrics, auto-kinetics, mocoles, motorigs and locomobiles.)

DRINK A BOTTLE OF CARBONATED Coca-Cola 5 CENTS — THE MOST REFRESHING DRINK IN THE WORLD.

Songs and 'The Shimmy'

The popular songs of the "Gay Nineties" were sentimental, religious or both, but there was a whole lot of secular shaking going on. The British music hall song "Ta-ra-ra boom-de-ay" became a U. S. favorite as well, jostling for attention with "Oh Promise Me" and "The Rosary."

"After the Ball is Over" sold by the thousands, along with "There'll Be a Hot Time in Old Town Tonight" and "On the Banks of the Wabash."

The Chicago Columbian Exposition introduced a dance called "The Hootchy Kootchy" that would become better known as "The Shimmy."

There was more ferment in New Orleans and St. Louis as Jelly Roll Morton and Scott Joplin explored new frontiers of jazz and ragtime.

Art in Ferment

Modern art was a horror called Impressionism and made worse by the works of Cezanne, Van Gogh and Gauguin. Concert halls and parlor pianos sampled the new music of Tchaikovsky and Dvorak; ears were outraged by Debussy's *Afternoon of a Faun.* Theatregoers bristled at the plays of Ibsen, laughed at Oscar Wilde's comedies, were puzzled by the wit of Shaw.

It was a decade of landmarks.

1890—Ibsen's *Hedda Gabler;* Wilde's *The Picture of Dorian Gray;* Strauss' *Death and Transfiguration;* Mascagni's *Cavalleria Rusticana.*

1891—Hardy's *Tess of the D'Urbervilles;* Kipling's *The Light That Failed;* Van Gogh's canvases exhibited posthumously; Toulouse-Lautrec begins his series of music hall posters; Mahler finishes his first symphony, Rachmaninoff his first concerto.

1892—Shaw's *Mrs. Warren's Profession;* Wilde's *Lady Windermere's Fan;* Monet begins Rouen Cathedral series; Toulouse-Lautrec's *Moulin Rouge;* Tchaikovsky's *Nutcracker;* Leoncavallo's *Pagliacci.*

1893—Dvorak's *New World Symphony* premieres.

1894—Shaw's *Arms and the Man;* Sibelius' *Finlandia.*

1895—H. G. Wells' *The Time Machine;* Tchaikovsky's *Swan Lake.*

1896—Chekhov's *The Sea Gull;* Strauss' *Zarathustra;* Puccini's *La Boheme.*

1897—Kipling's *Captains Courageous;* Shaw's *Candida;* Rodin's *Victor Hugo;* paintings by Henri Rousseau and Matisse.

1898—Henry James' *The Turn of the Screw;* H. G. Wells' *The War of the Worlds;* Arturo Toscanini debuts at La Scala.

1899—Wilde's *The Importance of Being Earnest;* Strauss' *Heldenleben.*

9

20th Century Unlimited

The 20th Century kicked up its heels to the cakewalk and rushed to discover wheels and speed, giddy with a new sense of motion and freedom. The century of electricity had begun: Electric lights were no longer feared as a fire hazard; they were even in the White House. Patents were issued for electric air conditioners and washing machines.

Thanks in part to such labor- and time-saving devices, more women were at work than ever. Though the hit song of 1905 was a ditty called "Everybody Works But Father," some men—their jobs lost to women—were not amused.

Women hiked their skirts a few inches off the floor and shortened their hair. "The Gibson Girl" look was an ideal often copied, seldom duplicated.

There was a dark side being probed by Freud and a dark cloud hanging over Einstein's $E = mc^2$, but few were alarmed for few understood either "The Interpretation of Dreams" or "The Theory of Relativity."

There was a lighter, brighter side as well: songs like "In the Good Old Summertime," "Bill Bailey Won't You Please Come Home" and "If You Talk in Your Sleep, Don't Mention My Name!"

The first experimental broadcast of voice and music was beamed on Christmas Eve 1906, but few heard it. More intriguing were the opening of nickelodeons in 1905, and the premiere of "The Great Train Robbery" two years before, and the screening of "Gertie the Dinosaur," the first cartoon, in 1909.

The birthrate and the rate of immigration rose in tandem. The numbers were fascinating: The population passed 75 million; there were 1,335,911 telephones in use, and 4,000 motorcars. Never mind that there were still 18 million horses and mules: The future had arrived with Henry Ford's mass-produced Model T.

And as Ford himself said: "You could have it in any color as long as it was black."

A Century in Motion

1900—Max Planck elaborates quantum theory; first trial flight of Zeppelin.

1901—First motor-driven bicycles; William Maybach constructs first Mercedes car.

1903—Orville and Wilbur Wright make first successful flight of a heavier-than-air machine at Kitty Hawk, N.C; Henry Ford organizes the Ford Motor Company; first coast-to-coast crossing of U.S. continent by auto (time: 65 days).

1904—First Vanderbilt Cup auto race (a Mercedes won); steerage rates for immigrants to America reduced to $10; work begins on Panama Canal.

1906—U.S. auto-makers produce 23,000 cars; French Grand Prix motor race first held.

1907—S.S. Lusitania breaks transatlantic record: Ireland to New York in 5 days, 45 minutes.

1908—General Motors Corporation formed; Wilbur Wright flies 30 miles in 40 minutes; Ford produces first Model T (cost: $950).

1909—Ford adapts assembly line to manufacture Model T (eventual sales: 15 million).

1910—Halley's Comet, last seen in 1835, the year of Mark Twain's birth, passes the sun again in the year of Twain's death. Halley predicted its next appearance in 1985.

The Birth of a Bottle

Designer Raymond Loewy called the famous bottle "the most perfectly designed package in use today." Others have commented that its double appeal to hand and eye "firmly establishes a tactile and visual sense relationship with the product." They confirm what anybody who's ever held a bottle of Coca-Cola immediately knows: To hold one is to see one.

It was not always so. The first bottle of Coke was a Hutchinson soda water bottle with an iron stopper and rubber washer attached. (The popping sound made by Hutchinson bottles probably gave "soda pop" its name.) It was bottled by the Joseph Biedenharn Candy Company of Vicksburg, Mississippi, which also supplied its customers with soda water bought from a Vicksburg bottling firm.

Imagine a hot Mississippi summer and a July 4th picnic with nothing cool to drink. Biedenharn had ordered extra cases of soda water for three big plantation picnics, but his usual supplier couldn't keep up with its own orders. Biedenharn delivered lemons, sugar and food coloring for pink lemonade — along with apologies. Before the end of 1894, Biedenharn bought one of Vicksburg's two bottling firms, determined not to disappoint his customers the following Fourth.

Since Biedenharn had done well with Coca-Cola at his confectionary's soda fountain, he decided to bottle Coca-Cola in addition to the customary plain sodas or fruit flavors. There was no contract, not even a consultation with Asa Candler, though the Biedenharns sent him two wooden cases of their bottled Coke. His only recorded response: "It was fine."

Bottling became a full-scale enterprise within a decade after Biedenharn's inspiration, but not until Benjamin Thomas and Joseph Whitehead, from Chattanooga, Tennessee, persuaded Candler to grant them bottling rights.

They were given a simple, 600-word contract — in perpetuity — to bottle enough Coke to supply demands for it without expense or liability to The Coca-Cola Company, to buy the syrup at a fixed price per gallon and not interfere with soda-fountain sales.

Thomas and Whitehead were to pay Candler the total sum of $1 for what turned out to be one of the world's most lucrative pacts. The Coca-Cola Company records indicate the dollar was never collected.

Bottling operations cost between $3,000 and $5,000 — expensive in 1900 dollars — and demand for Coca-Cola in bottles outgrew Thomas and Whitehead's ability to supply it. Thomas and Whitehead (who had formed a partnership with John Lupton) divided their territory — virtually all of the United States (New England was covered by a jobber's contract, Texas was

Joseph A. Biedenharn, age 28, bottled Coca-Cola in Vicksburg, Mississippi, in 1894.

A Chronology

1886—J. S. Pemberton creates Coca-Cola.
1891—Asa Candler acquires 100 per cent interest in Coca-Cola.
1892—"The Coca-Cola Company" is formed. Capital stock: $100,000.
1893—"Coca-Cola" trademark registered with U.S. Patent Office.
1894—Biedenharn Candy Co. in Vicksburg, Miss., begins bottling Coca-Cola, using fountain syrup. Sales limited to immediate area.
—First plant for manufacturing syrup outside Atlanta is established in Dallas, Tex.
1895—Syrup plants open in Chicago and Los Angeles.
1899—Bottling rights granted to Benjamin Thomas and Joseph Whitehead to bottle and sell Coca-Cola (except in Mississippi, Texas and the New England states). First bottling plant opens, in Chattanooga.
1900—Thomas and Whitehead divide their territory. Thomas organizes The Coca-Cola Bottling Co. (Thomas), Inc. Whitehead moves to Atlanta, where the second bottling plant is established.
1909—*The Coca-Cola Bottler* magazine begins publication.
1915—After Harold Hirsch, a counselor for The Coca-Cola Company, urges adoption of uniform bottle and Alexander Samuelson designs new container, Root Glass Co. patents it. Bottlers approve design following year.
1919—For $25 million, Candler family sell interests to group represented by banker Ernest Woodruff.
1921—Perpetuity of Bottler contracts affirmed by courts.
1923—Ernest's son Robert W. Woodruff assumes leadership of The Coca-Cola Company.
1928—Bottle sales exceed fountain sales for first time.
1930—Mechanically referigerated coolers introduced.
1935—Coin-operated vending machines put in use.
1942—Excepting the "Thomas Company" bottling operations, The Coca-Cola Company acquires the last of the original Parent Bottlers as a wholly owned subsidiary.
1955—King and Family size bottles introduced. Coke packaged in cans for first time; distribution limited to U.S. armed forces in Far East.
1964—The Coca-Cola Company introduces lift-top cans and crown, firsts in soft-drink industry.

tentatively promised, and the Biedenharns held on to Mississippi for a few years).

Would-be bottlers were courted, screened, signed. By 1919 there were more than 1,000 U.S. bottlers, supplied by four "Parent" bottling companies: The Coca-Cola Bottling Company, headquartered in Atlanta; The Coca-Cola Bottling Company (1903), in Dallas, Texas; the Western Coca-Cola Bottling Company, Chicago; and The Coca-Cola Bottling Company (Thomas) Inc., in Chattanooga. The Coca-Cola Company has since acquired all the Parent Bottlers.

There was, however, the problem of finding a unique "package": a bottle so distinctive that it would be recognized by a person as a bottle of Coca-Cola "when he feels it in the dark," as Benjamin Thomas said.

By 1913, Harold Hirsch, attorney for The Coca-Cola Company, urged developing a uniform bottle. Alexander Samuelson designed it; his employers, The C. J. Root Glass Company, patented it in 1915. A year later, bottlers of Coca-Cola approved its adoption.

In 1960, the U.S. Patent Office entered the famous bottle as a trademark, a recognition granted to few "packages." But few packages have ever been so closely identified with the products they contain.

The first site of the Atlanta Coca-Cola Bottling Company, 125 Edgewood Avenue, still stands near the downtown campus of Georgia State University.

The Handy Bottlers Wagon

Do you want a *Coca-Cola* Contract?

A few fine openings for *Coca-Cola* bottlers in the Northwest

MANUFACTURED BY
Gold Seal Ginger Ale
WESTERN COCA COLA BOTTLING CO., CHICAGO ILL.

Western Coca-Cola Bottling Company
1420 Masonic Temple
CHICAGO

'Teens and After:

Drink
Coca-Cola
Delicious and Refreshing

The Coca-Cola Company, Atlanta, Ga.

6,000,000 A DAY
In fact, Coca-Cola has an average sale of more than six million drinks for every day in the year ~ It has the charm of purity.

RE~FRESH YOURSELF! FIVE CENTS IS THE PRICE

This magazine ad appeared in May, 1925.

Robert Winship Woodruff once claimed, "I didn't know any more about Coke then than a pig knows about Sunday." What he did know was how to organize and merchandize—and drive a shrewd bargain.

As a youngster he was given a 50-cent weekly allowance to feed the horse he rode to school. He made friends with the stableman who tended horses near his school. Asa Candler, who had been one of young Woodruff's Sunday-school teachers, owned the stable. The stableman fed the horse; Woodruff pocketed the 50 cents.

Bored by school, Woodruff dropped out of Emory College (supported by the Candlers and later by Woodruff). His father insisted that the son pay his college debts; the younger Woodruff did so from his 60-cents-a-day wages as an apprentice machinist in an Atlanta foundry.

Employed by the Atlantic Ice and Coal Company, also owned by his father, he replaced the company's horse-drawn wagons with a fleet of trucks bought from the White Motor Company. Owner Walter White, so impressed by the deal that Woodruff struck, hired him. Following White's accidental death in 1922, Woodruff

SAVE THE CARTON

Thirst knows no season

Drink
Coca-Cola
Delicious and Refreshing

In the Distinctive Bottle

The Coca-Cola Co.
ATLANTA, GA.

Asa Candler's 1917 Christmas gift to his family was The Coca-Cola Company. He had bought the product for $2,300 and built it into a multi-million dollar business. In 1919, Candler's children sold The Coca-Cola Company for $25 million. It was the largest financial transaction in the Southeast and a national and international news item.

Atlanta businessman Ernest Woodruff engineered its purchase, backed by the Trust Company of Georgia (he was its president) and two New York banks, Chase National and Guaranty Trust Company.

The Candlers were paid $15 million in cash and issued $10 million in preferred stock (retired by 1926). The newly organized company, incorporated in Delaware, issued 500,000 shares of stock, offered principally through the Trust Company Bank at $40 per share. Allowing for stock splits and dividends, one share of stock in The Coca-Cola Company bought in 1919 for $40 is worth more than $16,000 today.

But that dramatic escalation in value came after a cloudy beginning. World War I had driven the price of sugar to four times its pre-war cost. Between 1920 and 1922, sales of Coke dropped by almost 18 per cent. The price of a share of stock dropped from $40 to $18.

It was time for a change. Against his father Ernest's advice, Robert Woodruff was named president of The Coca-Cola Company in 1923. As a long-time executive of The Coca-Cola Company once said: "Candler put us on our feet, but Woodruff gave us wings."

Drink
Coca-Cola

Enter Woodruff

was appointed president of the firm. And when The Coca-Cola Company elected him president in 1923, he served for a year as president of both firms, commuting between Atlanta and Cleveland, Ohio.

Woodruff led The Coca-Cola Company to global status. His contributions included insistence that the product itself was more important than individual interests. His first letter to stockholders declared: "All of our equipment might be replaced more easily than could our good will . . . intrinsic worth of the product, good service in distribution, and vision for the future in the management are the safeguards of this good will."

Advertising and bottling were standardized. Bottling contracts were revised to allow for fluctuations in the cost of sugar; territorial bottling rights were protected, and contracts were reaffirmed as perpetual.

Advertising gave equal prominence to Coca-Cola in bottles, which soon surpassed soda-fountain sales. Electric coolers were introduced. Cartons were manufactured to encourage quantity purchases by home consumers. Woodruff insisted on the primacy of Coca-Cola — and in the uniform 6-ounce package. Mergers and acquisitions — and bigger bottles — would come later.

Atlanta's "Mr. Anonymous"

Starting with Asa Candler and Benjamin Thomas, those who've made fortunes from Coca-Cola have shared their wealth with schools, churches, hospitals and other community institutions.

None have been more generous than Robert Woodruff. For years his gifts to Atlanta were contributions made by an "anonymous donor." Only recently have most of those gifts been identified as Woodruff's.

They stem from five foundations and total more than $250 million. Among the recipients: The Atlanta Memorial Arts Center, Central City Park and other Atlanta parks, the Emory University Medical Center, Fernbank Science Center, the Martin Luther King Jr. Memorial, the Boys Clubs of America, Goodwill Industries, the Atlanta University Center, American Red Cross and the Y.M.C.A.

During his first year as president of The Coca-Cola Company, Robert W. Woodruff also served as president of the White Motor Company.

After Austin

J. Paul Austin became president of The Coca-Cola Company in 1959, guiding it into a multi-national, multi-faceted corporation. Minute Maid (orange juice and "Hi C" fruit drinks) was acquired in 1960; the Fanta Beverage Company was created in the same year and added Sprite to its flavors. Tab appeared in 1963, Fresca in 1966.

Duncan Foods (coffee and tea) was acquired in 1964; the Belmont Springs Water Company, processors of natural water, was added in 1969. Aqua-Chem, a major producer of water purification equipment, was acquired in 1970, the year Austin was elected Chairman of the Board as well as president of The Coca-Cola Company.

Yes, Good to the Last Drop

The Fame of the Name

When Coca-Cola was born, it competed with a rainbow of soda-fountain flavors. Within decades it was on everybody's lips—and advertising put it there.

By the time the Roaring Twenties found their raucous voice, The Coca-Cola Company had orchestrated a medley of ad techniques: ads in newspapers and magazines; streetcar cards, oilcloth signs, cotton signs, metal signs and signs painted on walls.

Hats, caps and aprons for soda fountain personnel (they wouldn't be called ''soda jerks'' until the Forties); and a cornucopia of stuff to make a collector's eyes pop quicker than the first bottles of Coke: paper weights, pocket knives, trays, calendars, clocks, thermometers, blotters, mirrors, door plates, pencils, watch fobs and wallets. And for delivery wagons still horse drawn, umbrellas spreading the name of Coca-Cola in the rain and under the sun. Then came billboards. Remember these?

1927—Around the corner from anywhere.	1949—Coca-Cola . . . along the highway to anywhere.
1932—Ice-cold sunshine.	1952—What you want is a Coke.
Thirst come, thirst served.	1955—Bright and bracing as sunshine.
1938—The best friend thirst ever had.	1956—Coca-Cola . . . makes good things taste better.
1939—Whoever you are, whatever you do, wherever you may be, when you think of refreshment, think of ice-cold Coca-Cola.	1957—Sign of good taste.
	1958—The cold, crisp taste of Coke.
1941—Work refreshed.	1963—Things go better with Coke.
1942—The only thing like Coca-Cola is Coca-Cola itself.	1970—It's the real thing.
It's the real thing.	1971—I'd like to buy the world a Coke.
	1976—Coke adds life. . .

of the Pause That Refreshes

Movies Go Better with Coke

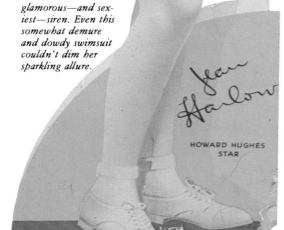

First there was opera star Lillian Nordica, then actress Hilda Clark.

Then came the movies and Pearl White, America's favorite damsel-in-distress.

Following audiences everywhere, ads for Coca-Cola became a fan club's delight: celebrities in magazine ads, starlets on billboards, actresses on trays, calendars and in life-size cutouts. All that was before refreshment stands and snack bars invaded movie lobbies.

Once Coca-Cola had literally gone to the movies, movies began to go better with Coke.

Steve McQueen graduated from TV cops-and-robbers roles to solid Hollywood hits.

Raquel Welch, above, pitched new white-on-red ribbony logo for 1970. At right, supporting actor pauses to refresh between takes of MGM's 1934 Merry Widow.

Paul Newman here pauses during pursuit of racing hobby. Films include greats like Hud, The Sting.

Until her death, at 26, in 1937, Jean Harlow was Hollywood's "Blonde Bombshell," the Thirties' most glamorous—and sexiest—siren. Even this somewhat demure and dowdy swimsuit couldn't dim her sparkling allure.

Dinner at Eight was a landmark among all-star films. Its giant cast included John and Lionel Barrymore, Marie Dressler, Wallace Beery, Jean Harlow, Billie Burke, May Robson, Lee Tracy, Edmund Lowe, Madge Evans and Jean Hersholt.

Burt Lancaster's first film was The Killers *in 1946. His growth as an actor is chronicled in memorable movies like* Elmer Gantry *(for which he won an Oscar),* Come Back Little Sheba, From Here to Eternity.

Marion Davies never became the star patron William Randolph Hearst hoped. Handful of films she made before her 1936 retirement included Little Old New York, Cain and Mabel, Ever Since Eve.

Jean Harlow inspired craze for platinum blondes. Her roles included Platinum Blond, Bombshell, Red Dust, Public Enemy, China Seas.

Maureen O'Sullivan was the Tarzan series' most famous Jane, Johnny Weismuller its most famous Tarzan. This 1934 filming break seems to add "You drink Coke" to oft-parodied "Me Tarzan, you Jane."

A Cinematic Calendar

1903—*The Great Train Robbery*
1905—Nickelodeons introduced
1909—*Gertie the Dinosaur,* first cartoon
1913—Hollywood becomes movie capital
1926—First experiments with sound effects and music
1927—Academy of Motion Picture Arts and Sciences; *The Jazz Singer,* first "talkie"
1928—*Lights of New York,* first all-talking picture; first Academy Awards (dubbed "Oscar" in 1931); first Mickey Mouse cartoons
1932—*La Cucaracha* introduces Technicolor

Lupe Velez, "The Mexican Spitfire."

Great American Pastimes

They've gone together so long, it's almost impossible to think of baseball without thinking of Coca-Cola. Some of the game's all-time heroes urged fans to follow their lead toward the great pastime's great refresher. (Ty Cobb was so convinced, he became a stockholder.)

But baseball's not the nation's *only* pastime—or that of Coke. The appeals of Coke—and ads—have gone for golf, tennis, football, basketball, racing, skiing (your choice of slope or wave). And don't forget the oars when two of you head for a canoe.

Live life refreshed, look for the best, look for the real thing. Coke.

Copyright © 1970, The Coca-Cola Company. "Coca-Cola" and "Coke" are registered trade-marks which identify the same product of The Coca-Cola Company.

It's Twice-Time!

Time to bring home two cartons of Coca-Cola in large sizes. Get twice the economy, twice the refreshment. You can't have too much Coke—because Coke has the taste you never get tired of. So don't run out. Stock up now.

For twice the economy, bring home two cartons of Coke in large sizes.

It's the real thing. Coke.

20

Pastime Peaks

1886—Amateur Golf Championship begins.
1890—James Naismith invents basketball.
1896—First modern Olympic games held in Athens, Greece.
1900—First Davis Cup tennis matches.
1903—First World Series.
1904—First perfect major league game; United States hosts its first Olympics.
1916—First professional golf tournament; first annual Rose Bowl football game.
1922—First play-by-play broadcast of World Series.
1930—Bobby Jones (later a Coca-Cola bottler) is first "grand-slam" golfer.
1936—Basketball first included among Olympic games.
1947—Jackie Robinson, first black major leaguer, joins Brooklyn Dodgers.
1948—Citation is first Kentucky Derby winner to earn more than $1 million.
1974—Hank Aaron hits his 715th home-run.
1978—Muhammad Ali is first three-time winner of heavyweight championship.

21

Flapper Finery

They were the Roaring Twenties, the Jazz Age, the years of the Flapper and Flaming Youth.

What did they sound like?

Listen to Louis Armstrong and Bix Beiderbecke. Or string a few songs together and hear singers who were just wild about Harry go looking for a silver lining while, in the meantime, in between time, insisting *Ain't We Got Fun?* Or throw yourself into a Charleston, knees knocking, heels flying, hips swinging, beads lurching around your neck or flared cuffs fanning your shoes.

Waists were back, skirts were up—*way* up—and stockings, sometimes, rolled down below the knee. To see what they looked like, browse a batch of fetching ads: The Twenties, like every other decade, were plain and fancy, outrageous and subdued, elegant fun and everyday functional.

AT A COOL AND CHEERFUL PLACE
You'll find a wonderful girl in a real
American pose – at the soda fountain
– When thirsty remember her.

The All-American (Liberated) Siren

The women in the ads, even at their most bare, were never a mere sex symbol. For one thing, the drink that tastes good was determined always to show good taste. For another, once they caught your eye, Coca-Cola was the symbol they celebrated.

Even some of the earliest ads were directed to women as well as men. She was always a lady, but often a learned one. That she was a reader was taken for granted: Book covers and magazines were adorned with ads inviting her to enjoy a Coke. Billboards and posters showed her at the theater, driving a car, playing tennis and golf.

She was sometimes contemplative, her eyes fixed in thought, her mouth curving into a smile prompted by an inner-sight of secret things.

She was fashionable, but never fashion's slave. She worked. She relaxed. She entertained. And when war came, she went to war.

And when she took the role of siren—always near water, always looking cool, always refreshed, Coke in hand—you *had* to have one too!

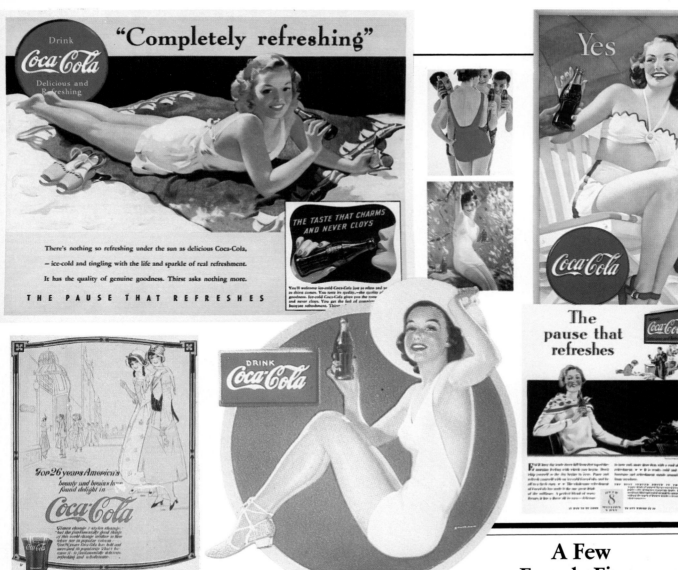

"Completely refreshing"

Drink **Coca-Cola** Delicious and Refreshing

Yes

There's nothing so refreshing under the sun as delicious Coca-Cola, — ice-cold and tingling with the life and sparkle of real refreshment.

It has the quality of genuine goodness. Thirst asks nothing more.

THE PAUSE THAT REFRESHES

THE TASTE THAT CHARMS AND NEVER CLOYS

For 26 years America's beauty and brains have found delight in **Coca-Cola**

DRINK **Coca-Cola**

The pause that refreshes

"The rest-pause that refreshes"

DRINK **Coca-Cola**

A Few Female Firsts

1888—Belva Ann Lockwood, first woman to argue a case before U.S. Supreme Court, becomes first woman to run for President when nominated by the Equal Rights Party.

1890—Wyoming becomes 44th state. As a territory, Wyoming had granted women the right to vote, thus was the first state to grant female suffrage.

1904—New York policeman makes first arrest of a woman for smoking in public in an open car. Said he: "You can't do that on Fifth Avenue." Some years later, actress Mrs. Patrick Campbell was asked by the Plaza Hotel's manager to put out her cigarette. Said she: "I have been given to understand this is a free country, and I propose to do nothing to alter its status."

1917—Jeannette Rankin is elected first woman member of the House of Representatives.

1920—The 19th Amendment, granting woman suffrage, is adopted.

1922—Rebecca Latimer Felton is appointed first female U.S. Senator.

1926—Gertrude Ederle, age 19, is first woman to swim English Channel.

1932—Amelia Earhart completes first transAtlantic flight by a woman pilot.

1963—Soviet astronaut Valentina Tereshkova, first woman in space, orbits the earth three times.

1978—Stella Taylor, attempting to swim from Bahamas to Florida, sets endurance record of 51 hours.

TAKE HOME A CARTON

DRINK
Coca-Cola

DRINK
Coca-Cola

The Thirsty Thirties

When they weren't the worst of times, the Thirties seemed the best of times. Unemployment was a global virus. The world stumbled toward war, hobbled by the weight of the Great Depression. "Brother, Can You Spare a Dime?" was the decade's theme song.

But there was another Thirties, an age of creation and discovery. America's best-sellers were classics in the making by Faulkner, Hemingway, Steinbeck, Fitzgerald, Dos Passos, Pearl Buck, Katherine Anne Porter and Margaret Mitchell.

Broadway was hatching songs by George Gershwin, Cole Porter, Irving Berlin, Jerome Kern, Rodgers and

Thirties Things

1930—*The Star Spangled Banner* is declared the national anthem. The planet Pluto is discovered.
1932—Franklin D. Roosevelt elected to first of four terms; expression "New Deal" is first used in his acceptance speech.
1933—Prohibition repealed.
1935—Italy invades Ethiopia.
  Gershwin writes *Porgy and Bess.*
  The "Swing" era begins.
1936—Spanish Civil War begins.
  Edward VIII abdicates his throne for "the woman I love"; is named Duke of Windsor; marries Mrs. Wallis Simpson in 1937. Margaret Mitchell publishes *Gone with the Wind. Is It True What They Say About Dixie?* is a hit song.
1937—Amelia Earhart lost on Pacific flight.
1939—John Steinbeck publishes *The Grapes of Wrath.* World War II begins.

Hart. Hollywood was in its golden age. Radio had become a livingroom theater/concert hall/newsroom whose greatest gift may have been the laughter of Fred Allen, Jack Benny, Fibber McGee, Bob Hope, Edgar Bergen and Charlie McCarthy, and Burns and Allen.

The lights were being turned on in every American city and town. Illiteracy had dropped to an all-time low. Population passed 120 million; and despite hard times, there was material evidence of the good life: 19 million cars; 2 million household refrigerators.

And inside them, getting very cold, were bottles of Coca-Cola counted at the rate of 9 million a day.

The Biggest Nickel's Worth In The Store

That's what people say about Coca-Cola—because it is so good. And more people buy Coca-Cola than buy any other drink—because when served ice-cold in the regular Coca-Cola glass it delights taste and satisfies thirst as nothing else can.

Stick at exercise and you'll keep a slim figure. And *the pause that refreshes* with ice-cold Coca-Cola will cheer you along . . . Its life and sparkle will awaken energy and make the going easier. It's the drink that keeps you feeling fit for what's ahead.

The pause that keeps you going – keeping a slim figure

27

The Broadcast Boom

They were more than voices. They were like family who came to visit every week—sometimes every evening. As in all families, problems sometimes surfaced: Who, when two favorites opposed each other, would be tuned in?

Whatever the choice, tuned in America *was*—and turned *on*. There was Beethoven by Toscanini, Brahms by Stokowski, Gershwin by Paul Whiteman. There were Broadway stars, Hollywood stars and a jamboree of jazz masters. There was the wit of *Information Please* and the trivia of Robert Ripley's *Believe It or Not*. The spine-chilling menace of *Inner Sanctum* and *Lights Out*. The grim reality of H. V. Kaltenborn and Edward R. Murrow broadcasting from a continent lurching toward war.

Beyond entertainment and information, radio became a wireless bond that, while broadcasting even the most harrowing happenings of World War II, reminded Americans that we were committed to and with one another.

Charlie McCarthy and the Sprite were go-together pixies who made the transition from radio to TV with ease. Bergen's dummy, no dummy in front of a mike, was a master of splintery jibes. His repartee with such comics as W. C. Fields produced classic moments. Charlie to Fields: "I'll mow you down!" Fields to McCarthy: "Go 'way or I'll sic a woodpecker on you."

Bergen, McCarthy and Mortimer Snerd made more than a dozen films together. Bergen, an accomplished actor, appeared without his friends in the memorable movie I Remember Mama.

Listeners' Choice

When station KDKA made the first commercial broadcast in 1920, there were about 5,000 radios in America. By 1940, when such events as Franklin Roosevelt's election to a third term were broadcast, the number had risen to 30 million. Radio's almost hypnotic appeal was strengthened by its variety. During a single week in 1938, listeners could choose from these typical offerings:

Comedy: *Amos 'n' Andy, Easy Aces, Fibber McGee and Molly, Jack Benny, Burns and Allen*, Fannie Brice and Edgar Bergen.

Dramatic series: *Gangbusters, Grand Central Station, The Green Hornet, Death Valley Days, One Man's Family* and *Mr. Keen, Tracer of Lost Persons*. Performers in dramatic specials included Claire Trevor, Tyrone Power, Edward G. Robinson and Robert Taylor.

Musical shows: Connie Boswell, Bing Crosby, Kate Smith, Tony Martin and Rudy Vallee were featured soloists. Orchestras included Duke Ellington, Paul Whiteman, Tommy Dorsey, Kay Kyser, Andre Kostelanetz, Russ Morgan, Wayne King and Phil Spitalny's All Girl Orchestra.

*Petula Clark made hit discs in the Sixties,
then moved into film singing roles
(Finian's Rainbow; Goodbye, Mr. Chips).*

*Diana Ross, here with
Supremes, became movie
superstar.*

A Dial of Dates

1891—Thomas Edison awarded first important radio patent for "a means of transmitting signals electrically . . . without the use of wires."

1900—First voice broadcast transmitted by American scientist R. A. Fessenden.

1906—Fessenden broadcasts first U. S. radio program of voice and music.

1909—First wireless message sent from New York to Chicago.

1920—Station KDKA in East Pittsburgh, Pa., begins first national radio service, broadcasting returns of Harding-Cox election.

1922—Station WEAF, New York, broadcasts first U. S. commercially sponsored program.

1937—First coast-to-coast broadcast is Herbert Morrison's description of the landing and explosion of the *Hindenburg* at Lakehurst, N. J.; first world-wide radio broadcast heard in America covers the coronation of Britain's George VI.

1938—Orson Welles' radio drama, "Invasion from Mars," based on H. G. Wells' *The War of the Worlds,* causes widespread panic when listeners believe reports of a Martian invasion are true.

1960—Pioneer V transmits signals from 22.5 million miles in space.

*The McGuire Sisters—
Christine, Dorothy and
Phyllis.*

Tuning in TV

1925—Scottish inventor John Logie Baird transmits recognizable human features by TV.

1927—First successful demonstration of TV in America: In New York City, A. T. & T. president spoke with and saw Secretary of Commerce Herbert Hoover in Washington, D. C.

1928—Station WGY, Schenectady, N. Y., begins first program of scheduled TV broadcasts.

1941—Station WNBT, New York City, begins first commercial telecasts in United States.

1950—U. S. TV sets in use estimated at 1,500,000.

1951—First transcontinental telecast in United States: President Harry S. Truman, speaking in San Francisco, broadcast nationally on 94 U. S. stations.

1953—First experiments of TV color in United States.

1954—U. S. TV sets in use reaches 29 million — 3 out of 5 households.

1959—Quiz show scandals.
36 million sets in use.

1960—Kennedy-Nixon debates.
85 million sets in use.

1962—Satellite Telstar launched from Cape Canaveral, enabling trans-atlantic transmission.

1965—Early Bird, U. S. commercial communications satellite, first used by TV networks.

1970—Estimated 200 million sets in use worldwide.

*The Great Ray Charles,
master of music: His repertory
ranges from blues to rhythm
and blues, from rock to jazz,
from bluegrass to ballads.
Georgia On My Mind, Drown
in My Own Tears and his own
What'd I Say are among the
singer's summit sessions.*

A Coke by Any Other Name

"WAS IST COCA-COLA?"

The question's rarely asked these days, either in Germany or the many other countries where you don't have to know the language to order a Coke.

It might help to recognize the famous bottle or the famed bottle cap—or the fluid white-on-red symbol of the Seventies—but whether you're in Tel Aviv or Tasmania, the answer to "WAS IST COCA-COLA?" remains the same: "Das Weltbekannte Warenzeichen fur das einzigartige Erfrischungsgetrank der Coca-Cola." One sip translates for the sipper: "The world-famous trademark for the unique refreshment-beverage of Coca-Cola."

In 1898, Asa Candler informed his board of directors that Coca-Cola was shipped to and sold in Canada and Honolulu, and that arrangements were under way for shipments to Mexico. By the mid-Seventies, world sales exceeded 200 million 8-ounce servings daily.

DRINK **Coca-Cola** ICE COLD TRADE MARK REG.

English

BUVEZ **Coca-Cola** GLACÉ MARQUE DÉPOSÉE

French

TRINK **Coca-Cola** EISKALT WARENZEICHEN

German

DRIKK **Coca-Cola** ISKALD REG. VAREMERKE

Norwegian

TOME **Coca-Cola** BIEN FRÍA MARCA REG.

Spanish

Πίνετε **Coca-Cola** Παγωμένη

Greek

BEVETE **Coca-Cola** GHIACCIATA MARCHIO REG.

Italian

BEBA **Coca-Cola** BEM GELADA MARCA REG.

Portuguese

ดื่ม **Coca-Cola** เย็นเจี๊ยบ

Thai

請飲 **可口可樂** DRINK **Coca-Cola** TRADE MARK REG.

Chinese

飲みましょう **コカ・コーラ** 登録商標 DRINK **Coca-Cola**

Japanese

કોકા-કોલા **Coca-Cola**

Gujarati

ኮካ ኮላ **Coca-Cola** ንግድ ምልክት

Amharic

اشرب **Coca-Cola** كوكاكولا DRINK

Arabic

"Alto para refrescarse ...y con Coca-Cola"

Usted, como millones de personas más, ha de aclamar esta bebida deliciosa de cualidades únicas. Para refrescarse no hay nada mejor que Coca-Cola. Le agradará su sabor exquisito – pídala bien fría.

Tome **Coca-Cola** MARCA REGISTRADA Deliciosa y Refrescante

EMBOTELLADA BAJO CONTRATO CON THE COCA-COLA CO. POR

International Datelines

1899—First shipment of Coca-Cola to Cuba.

1900—Asa Candler's son Howard carries a gallon of syrup on a trip to Europe. He discovers a London soda fountain operated by an American who samples the drink and places an order for five gallons of syrup.

1901—Shipments to Jamaica begin. The Cola-Coca Company orders ad materials from Germany and begins selling syrup to German wholesalers.

1905—"Cola-Coca" registered as a trademark in Canada.

1906—Bottling plants built in Cuba and Panama, the first outside continental United States. A plant to bottle Coca-Cola is established in Canada, first country outside United States to manufacture syrup.

1912—San Miguel Brewery, Manila, sells Coca-Cola in the Philippines.

1926—Robert Woodruff organizes a "Foreign Department" in Manhattan.

1928—Coca-Cola bottled in China.

1929—Coca-Cola bottled by 64 firms in 28 foreign countries.

1930—Woodruff establishes a subsidiary, The Coca-Cola Export Corporation and is appointed its president (continuing as president of The Coca-Cola Company).

1938—Export Corp. opens Pan American Division.

1939—Seven bottlers in the British Isles; one each in Scotland and Northern Ireland.

1946—The 155 bottling plants operating around the world include 64 shipped from the United States between 1943 and 1946.

1978—Coca-Cola is bottled by 1,200 plants in 135 countries.

Tómese **Coca-Cola**

No hay refresco mejor, Fabricado en una planta higiénica y limpia y siendo sus componentes de primera calidad.

Le calma la sed y tonifica el cuerpo.

Fíjese bien en la botellita y en la tapa. Rechaze las imitaciones.

Se vende en todas partes à seis centavos la botella.

The Coca-Cola Company
Habana

frischwärts

Drink Coca-Cola

DRINK **Coca-Cola**

Delicious and Refreshing to the world

THE COCA-COLA COMPANY

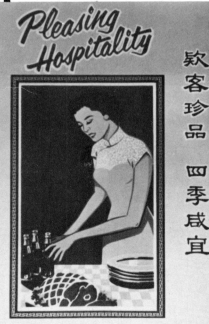

Pleasing Hospitality

歓客珍品 四季咸宜

WHERE THERE IS COCA-COLA—THERE IS HOSPITALITY

The Art of Coca-Cola

ART NOUVEAU was the dominant European decorative style of the 1890s. It stemmed from the fluid lines of posters by Toulouse-Lautrec, lamps and vases by Tiffany, crystal by Lalique. In the century since Art Nouveau first curved into view, it has had several revivals among decorators and designers. These panels from 1922, promoting Coca-Cola as a year-round beverage, are an echo of the no longer new Nouveau style.

IMPRESSIONISM is admired, even loved, 100 years after it assaulted the eyes of late-19th Century Parisians. It was a new way of seeing as well as painting. The style's originators, Claude Monet among them, sought to put onto canvas the world as seen—an impression of reality emerging from particles of color and vibrations of light.

By the Twenties, Impressionism had been tamed and even translated into commercial art, as in this treatment of the New York skyline in a 1920 ad.

POP ART was meant to be "as sweet and stupid as life itself." It took its images from America's street furniture: signs, neon, supermarket displays and billboards, billboards, billboards.

The famed bottle became a recurrent symbol in the works of Warhol, Rauschenberg, Mel Ramos, Escobar Marisol and James Dine. The Coca-Cola Company discourages such borrowings of its trademarks, but stimulated the movement.

With such premiums as this likeness of Aretha Franklin, Coca-Cola made its own contributions to the post-Pop poster craze.

Coca-Cola, too, is compatible with a well balanced diet. As a pure, wholesome drink, it provides a bit of quick energy...brings you back refreshed after work or play. It contributes to good health by providing a pleasurable moment's pause from the pace of a busy day.

After the prom...it's Coke Time

Ice-cold Coca-Cola has the taste you never get tired of. It's always refreshing. That's why things go better with Coke after Coke after Coke.

NEW WAVE? *For half a century "fine" and "commercial" art have fed and borrowed from each other. This simple 1960 ad, as subtle as an Old Master in its clarity and harmony of form, could herald canvases to come.*

THE ARRANGEMENT *of perpendiculars within a lean language of color marks the modern movement called* De Stijl *("The Style"). During the Fifties, American designers turned to the techniques of Piet Mondrian, The Style's most distinguished stylist. Cigarette packages, wrapping paper, wall coverings—even dresses and neckties—and, sometimes, the ads reflected the return of De Stijl's distinctive style.*

NEW- OR SUPER-REALISM *imitates the camera in its insistence on capturing the exactness of things. Life-size, but often larger than life, it seldom matches the real thing. The camera still does it better.*

MINIMAL ART *limits itself to the minimal realities of color and form and linear flow. The famous flowing white-on-red 1970 logo is a lyrical example of such reductions of painting to the very elements of art.*

DECORATIVE *gives "Art Deco" its name. American designers and architects—soon joined by painters and sculptors—translated what the French called* art moderne *into the "modernistic art" of the decades 1920 to 1940. The style was sleek and lean, almost an answer to Art Nouveau's curves and coils, and was revived in the Seventies by those attracted to its slightly exotic appeal.*

33

Wherever You Are, Whatever You Do...

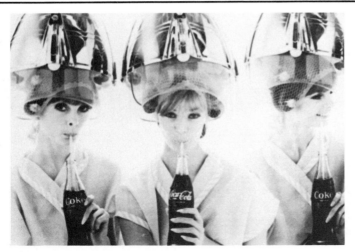

Coca-Cola was always for everybody.

When its commercials, billboards, magazine ads, supermarket displays, soda fountain festoons and calendars sang "Wherever you are, whatever you do, wherever you may be—when you think of refreshment, think of Coca-Cola," Coke had already created its audience.

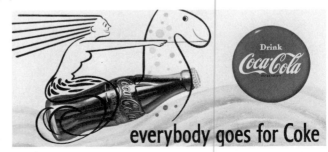

everybody goes for Coke

Whoever you are, whatever you do,
wherever you may be–

when you think of refreshment,
think of Coca-Cola

For Coca-Cola makes any pause
the pause that refreshes
and ice-cold Coca-Cola is everywhere

Coca-Cola "Coke" 5¢

DRINK Coca-Cola
DELICIOUS & REFRESHING

Coca-Cola
Sales for 1904 4,433,787 Gallons
showing it is valued and
appreciated by all classes

Reflections in a Glass:

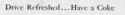

"Fashion reflects an era," says designer Norman Norell. "If, 2,000 years from now, people want to know about us, they'll look at our clothes."

End of the 20th or end of the 40th Century, the best place to look is in a collection of these ads, reflecting American fashions in a tinted bottle if not always in a golden eye.

Since, especially in fashions, the more things change the more they return to being the same, consider these ins-and-outs of styles that surfaced, submerged and came back up for air.

Forties' females softened the severity of the war years with sportswear and casual clothes—including the soon to become ubiquitous "T" shirt—but the square and padded-shoulder look stayed for awhile. Carmen Miranda platforms were reduced to "wedgies;" her fantastic headwear inspired "silly hats" and "mad little hats."

For the Fifties there were lists of fashion do's-and-

The best is always the better buy

36

Fashion Since the Forties

don't's. Among the do's were A-line dresses and dirndl skirts, stiffened crinolines and "little flatties" from Capezio. Short hair, pedal pushers and bigger hats were in, and by 1957 there was the "sack."

High school and college girls wore long tweed skirts with cardigans and bobby sox. Few fashion conformists dared flirt with such "beatnik"-inspired innovations as black stockings.

The Sixties brought Jackie Kennedy's little pillbox hats, but rebellious kids toward the end of the decade copied the Beatles' long locks.

By the Seventies, American fashion had become what you choose to wear, and the more functional by day the more fun costumes became by night. Young women invested in $200 silk blouses by Yves St. Laurent, wearing them, if they pleased, with jeans. After all, even St. Laurent declared that a personal style, once found, should never change.

Stitches in Time

1891—Zipper patented by Whitcomb L. Judson.

1901—Rayon commercially manufactured.

1906—Permanent wave machine invented and used in France.

1907—Electric washing machine patented.

1913—Ragtime introduces "Animal Dances": fox trot, horse trot, crab step, kangaroo dip, camel walk, fish walk, chicken scratch, lame duck, snake, grizzly bear, turkey trot, bunny hop. Irene and Vernon Castle help popularize the fox trot; hobble skirts are slit to knee to accommodate dancers.

1917—Fashion adopts a "mannish" look as women volunteer for World War I duties as clerks, drivers, nurses.

1922—Emily Post publishes *Etiquette: The Blue Book of Social Usage*.

1925—Gabrielle "Coco" Chanel's "little black dress" becomes popular.

1939—Nylon stockings, patented in 1937, sold in America for first time; fashion enters the Sears Roebuck catalogue with dresses "inspired by Schiaparelli."

1947—Christian Dior's "New Look" lowers skirts, pinches waists and flattens bosoms.

1949—Bikinis make waves on American beaches.

1950—Ballet flats, renamed "ballerinas," are worn by teenagers.

1955—Elvis Presley, *Rock Around the Clock*, and the semi-fitted sheath are the rage.

1957—Russians orbit the first Sputnik; American women wear their first "sacks."

Coca-Cola Goes to War

Your Glass of Coca-Cola represents materials allotted and authorized by Mr. Hoover and your Government after conservation has taken its heavy toll. The Coca-Cola Company accepts its war duty as a privilege and, although reduced in output, is endeavoring to maintain its usefulness as industry.

We address ourselves to common justice in requesting you, if you order Coca-Cola, to insist upon the genuine. Don't let a subtle imitation creep in to take advantage of our shortened output by passing itself off as a substitute.

When you order, order by its full name —Coca-Cola, and accept nothing else.

To the Dealer:

If you are unable sometimes to get Coca-Cola or always to get your full quota, we ask you to bear with us, remembering that your troubles are ours, in trying to supply normal trade with a restricted output—and remembering that the sacrifice for conservation must fall on all of us alike—dealer, manufacturer and consumer.

THE COCA-COLA CO., ATLANTA, GA.

More than 2 million U.S. troops fought in World War I. Most of the estimated 100 million other Americans thought of themselves as home-front fighters, equally committed, in the words of Woodrow Wilson, "to make the world safe for democracy."

All things German were banned, including the music of Beethoven (his *Fifth Symphony* would give World War II its *ta-ta-ta-tum*, V-for-Victory motif). Sauerkraut was called "liberty cabbage"; hamburger steak became "liberty steak," and dachshunds were "liberty pups."

Movie theaters offered patriotic sing-alongs, adding "Keep the Home Fires Burning" and "Pack Up Your Troubles" to such standards as "When Johnny Comes Marching Home" and "America."

The U.S. Food Board (headed by Herbert Hoover) declared "meatless" meals and "wheatless" days. Sugar was limited to two pounds per person per month. Gasoline consumption was cut voluntarily.

Manufacturers were asked to reduce production using vital materials (sugar included) by half. With that The Coca-Cola Company responded with full-page newspaper ads headed "Making a Soldier of Sugar."

During World War II rationing was more strict: sugar, gasoline, shoes, coffee, canned goods, meat. The Coca-Cola Company reprinted its 1917 ad, adding that sugar had "enlisted" for Victory. Its conclusion: "Whatever any of us may have, or may not have, Victory we must have above all else!"

Even bottles went to war: This one served as an electrical insulator, used by Seabees during World War II.

Gen. Jonathan Wainwright, hero of Bataan, conquers a hot dog and Coke during a post-war Yankee Stadium conflict.

Coca-Cola was included on GI ration cards during World War II.

Keep the Home Fires Singing

During both World Wars, popular songs reflected America's moods. They were most often serious or sentimental, but sometimes made fun of even the worst furors.

World War I	World War II
Bring Back My Daddy to Me	*A Boy in Khaki, a Girl in Lace*
Goodbye Broadway, Hello France	*Der Fuehrer's Face*
Hail, Hail, the Gang's All Here	*Don't Sit Under the Apple Tree*
Hello, Central, Give Me No Man's Land	*with Anyone Else But Me*
Hinky Dinky Parlez Vous	*Every Time We Say Goodbye*
I Don't Know Where I'm Going But I'm on My Way	*A Fellow on a Furlough*
I May Be Gone for a Long Long Time	*G. I. Jive*
If He Can Fight Like He Can Love,	*I Don't Want to Walk Without You*
Good Night Germany	*I Left My Heart at the Stage Door Canteen*
I'm Gonna Pin My Medal on the Girl I Left Behind	*I'll Be Home for Christmas*
It's a Long Way to Tipperary	*I'll Be Seeing You*
K-K-K-Katy	*I'll Walk Alone*
Lorraine, My Beautiful Alsace Lorraine	*Keep 'em Flying*
Meet Me at the Station, Dear	*Lili Marlene*
Never Forget to Write Home	*Milkman Keep Those Bottles Quiet*
Oh! Frenchy	*My Guy's Come Back*
Oh, How I Hate to Get Up in the Morning	*Praise the Lord and Pass the Ammunition*
Oui, Oui, Marie	*Remember Pearl Harbor*
Over There	*Say a Prayer for the Boys Over There*
Send Me Away with a Smile	*That Soldier of Mine*
There's a Long, Long Trail	*They're Either Too Young or Too Old*
Till We Meet Again	*When the Lights Go on Again All Over the World*
When the Boys Come Home	*You'd Be So Nice to Come Home To*

Mom, the Flag and Apple Pie..

The Pause that Refreshes had become the Pause that Boosted Morale.

A young Sergeant wrote his parents in Kansas: "It's the little things, not the big things that the individual soldier fights for or wants so badly when away. It's the girl friend back home in a drug store over a Coke, or the juke box and the summer weather."

Like Kilroy, Coke followed America's GIs wherever they went: 64 overseas bottling plants were built (59 transported at government expense as a military priority), stretching from Iceland to Iran, from North Africa to the Pacific.

Before Coca-Cola reached the Solomon Islands, bot-

Sublimated Essence

"Coca-Cola is the sublimated essence of all that America stands for."—William Allen White

La moda Americana... Have a Coke

... or an American custom as seen in Italy

"Howdy, friend"

Christmas together... Have a Coca-Cola

...welcoming a fighting man home from the wars

Have a "Coke" = Good winds have blown you here

...a way to say "We are friends" to the Chinese

So glad to see you... Have a Coca-Cola

... or today's friendships help make the future

The American Girl

"First of all, I don't know exactly what democracy is, or the real, common-sense meaning of a republic. But as we used to talk things over in China, we all used to agree that we were fighting for The American Girl. She to us was America. Democracy, Coca-Cola, Hamburgers, Clean Places to Sleep, or The American Way of Life."— *God is My Co-Pilot*, by Col. Robert L. Scott

and Coca-Cola

tles received in food packages from home sold for $5; in Casablanca a bottle of Coke was sold for $10. One soldier wrote home that he had refused an offer of $100 for a bottle. It was, he said, more valuable than money.

In Italy, two GIs who'd been sent a couple of bottles of Coca-Cola from home shared one, raffled the other. At 25 cents a shot, the raffle finally netted $5,000.73 (the missing two cents was never accounted for), the proceeds earmarked for the children of battalion members killed in action.

Commenting that he was too overwhelmed to drink such a costly Coke, the winner said: "I'll just send it home and keep it a few years."

Gen. Douglas MacArthur "autographed" the first bottle of Coke produced after the recapture of the Philippines.

Every Man in Uniform

Well known illustrator James Montgomery Flagg was among the World War II artists used by The Coca-Cola Company.

"We will see that every man in uniform gets a bottle of Coca-Cola for five cents, wherever he is and whatever it costs." — Robert W. Woodruff, President of The Coca-Cola Company, 1941

"I Had a Coca-Cola"

"This day that was to mark the turning point in the Battle of the Philippines began for me with an incident that seemed of the greatest importance. In fact, so vital did it seem at the time that that night, upon my return to the tunnel after one of the most terrible days a man could ever experience, I wrote a detailed account of that day on my typewriter with a ribbon that could hardly make itself legible, and with trembling hands I added the important notation: 'I had a Coca-Cola.'

"There is no use attempting to explain how important that seemed to me. That day I had seen men blown to shreds; I had seen white-faced nurses drag themselves from the bloody debris of a bombed hospital; I had escaped death many times. All this paled and was forgotten before the miracle of a five-cent drink any American can buy at his corner store."—I Saw the Fall of the Philippines, by Gen. Carlos Romulo

---

"Send 10 Coca-Cola Bottling Plants"

"On early convoy request shipment three million bottled Coca-Cola, (filled), and complete equipment for bottling, washing, capping same quantity twice monthly. (CITE SSQMC-599). Preference as to equipment is 10 separate machines for installation in different localities, each complete for bottling twenty thousand bottles per day. Also sufficient syrup and caps for 6 million refills. Syrup, caps and sixty thousand bottles monthly should be an automatic supply . . . ."— From a top-secret cablegram sent by Gen. Dwight D. Eisenhower to High Command Headquarters in Washington, June 29, 1945. (The document was unclassified in 1966.)

Sgt. de Schneider (left) collects his $5,000 bottle of Coke.

Calendars for Coke

In the beginning, The Coca-Cola Company's calendars were delightful premiums. Since the beginning, they've become premium delights.

Early calendars can fetch as much as $2,000 from collectors. They'd be driven wild by a complete collection of such series as bathing beauties or those illustrated by Norman Rockwell.

Collectors' mouths may water for them, but the calendars were originally a clue for quenching thirst.

August is the Coolest Month

In retrospect, the advertising seems at times predictable: the icy bottle for the hottest months, the warmest fireside scene for Winter's chill. February? Valentines, for sure. October? Autumn leaves or Halloween scenes. December? You know who.

But in their day, the campaigns for Coke were bold and often experimental. The first year's free coupons tempted thirsts. Turn-of-the-century trays served the soda fountain's ornate heyday. Magazines reached housewives, theatergoers, businessmen, students.

Billboards became springboards for teasing a generation newly taken to wheels to look for the newest slogan. There were new ones almost monthly, a refreshing departure from less frequently changed wall-painted signs.

As sales of Coke in bottles increased, billboards gave them appropriate billing. By 1928, bottles sold more Coke than soda fountains served.

But a Coke was a Coke; its taste remained constant. The same ad could be used for bottle or glass.

Phrases and themes, models and scenes were swapped within a fixed framework.

The Coca-Cola Company believed its own "Thirst Knows No Season" pitch. It might be August, but ads were looking cool.

THE PAUSE THAT REFRESHES

The Birth of a Notion

In 1919, the ownership of The Coca-Cola Company changed. A reporter swapped newspapering for *The Atlanta Georgian* for a job with the D'Arcy Advertising Company, which began co-ordinating ads for Coke in 1906.

His name was Archie Laney Lee. Though few recognize his name, the slogans and symbols that he helped create for Coca-Cola are etched in everybody's memory.

Four years after Lee joined D'Arcy, Robert Woodruff was president of The Coca-Cola Company. Longtime friends Lee and Woodruff bounced ideas off each other, fed each other's imagination and shaped the notion that the soft drink's most valuable secret was its universality.

Billboards multiplied the message: Coca-Cola was everywhere—and it was for everybody to enjoy. The bottle, already outstripping fountain sales, got equal or star billing with the famous glass.

The best known phrase from the Lee/D'Arcy years is among the world's most recognized: "The pause that refreshes." The icy, elfin, smiling "Sprite" was Lee's idea, realized by artist Haddon Sundblom. And the Santa Claus who beams in most childhood imaginings was dreamed by Lee and fleshed by Sundblom. It was a dream to cherish.

Thirst knows no season

5¢

The Coca-Cola Company
Atlanta, Ga.

Days for Holidays

1894—Labor Day is made a legal holiday.

1907—First observance of Mother's Day.

1910—First celebration of Father's Day.

1921—Armistice Day, commemorating end of World War I, declared a legal holiday. Changed to Veterans Day in 1954 to honor all men and women who've served in America's armed forces.

1941—Thanksgiving Day returns to last Thursday in November after two-year experiment to add a week to Christmas shopping.

1978—First observance of Grandparents Day.

'Twas the Coke Before Christmas

The Santa Claus appearing in ads for Coke became world's Santa.

Archie Lee dreamed him. Haddon Sundbl painted him. Everybody loved him.

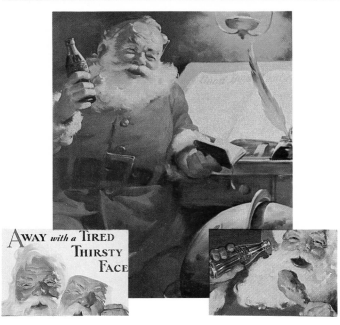

Hospitality in your refrigerator

Christmas time is hospitality time. For friendly visits and unexpected guests, the pause that refreshes with ice-cold Coca-Cola provides a gracious welcome. There's more Coke now, so keep an ample supply in your refrigerator for visitors, for your family, and for yourself.

It had to be good to get where it is

Drink Coca-Cola
Delicious and Refreshing

World's largest soda fountain in the great department store of Famous-Barr Co., St. Louis, where busy Christmas shoppers pause and refresh themselves with ice-cold Coca-Cola.

THE BUSIEST MAN IN THE WORLD
comes up smiling
after... *the pause that refreshes*

OF COURSE you find wonderful soda fountains in the great department stores. Even Old Santa, busiest man in the world, devotes a minute now and then to *the pause that refreshes.* It's a happy, sociable part of Christmas shopping—a little minute of rest and refreshment that gives you a fresh start. • • *The pause that refreshes,*

as everyone knows, is the short time it takes to enjoy an ice-cold Coca-Cola. The busier you are the more important it becomes. You relax, take a deep breath and quench your thirst with the tingling deliciousness of this pure drink of natural flavors. And, like Santa Claus himself, you come up smiling.

THE BEST SERVED DRINK IN THE WORLD
A pure drink of natural flavors served ice-cold in its own glass and in its own bottle. The crystal-thin Coca-Cola glass that represents the best in soda fountain service. The distinctive Coca-Cola bottle you can always identify; it is sterilized, filled and sealed air-tight without the touch of human hands, insuring purity and wholesomeness. The Coca-Cola Company, Atlanta, Ga.

LISTEN IN ⭢⭢ Grantland Rice ⭢⭢ Famous Sports Champions ⭢⭢ Coca-Cola Orchestra ⭢⭢ Wed. 10:30 to 11 p. m. Eastern Standard Time ⭢⭢ Coast to Coast N B C Network

© The Coca-Cola Company, 1930

NINE MILLION A DAY

Drink **Coca-Cola**
Delicious and Refreshing

things go
better
with
Coke

THE PAUSE THAT REFRESHES.

Toys, Trinkets and Treasures

Lucky kids!

Some recall when tablets, rulers, pencils, blotters and book covers—all featuring symbols of Coke—were the only cheerful things about the end of summer. The kids were what marketing analysts would call "future consumers," but that was beside the point. Who hadn't already sampled the dark delight?

Better yet were cardboard dioramas—circuses and miniature cities and a tiny Toonerville Trolley town. And for the pocket or purse, knives and mirrors and key chains.

For an age group yearning to be grown enough for wheels there were trucks and such, complete with Lilliputian crates, each with its own set of microscopic but exact bottles.

Like other memorabilia of Coca-Cola, these toys and trinkets have become treasures. And don't forget the grown-ups' pleasures: clocks and radios, shaped like cans or vending machines, music boxes made like coolers, the pocket-size bottles that flipped open to reveal cigarette lighters, watch fobs and jewelry, "T" shirts and scarves, trays and coasters, calendars, playing cards, posters and paper-weights . . .

Here's something special for the real times.

A Set of TV Trays illustrated with people and events in Black History . . . only $4.95.

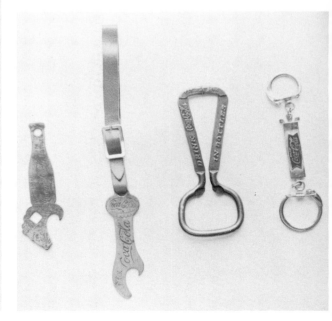

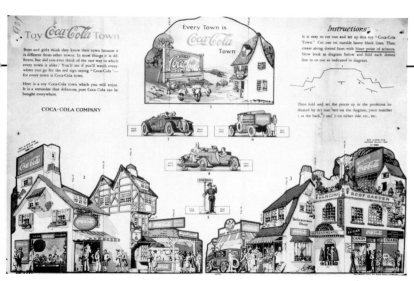

Toy Coca-Cola Town

Every Town is Coca-Cola Town

Instructions

After sewing—
After housework—
After play—

DRINK BOTTLED

Coca-Cola

DELICIOUS and REFRESHING

Keep it on ice for your family and your friends.

ORDER A CASE OF Coca-Cola FOR YOUR HOME

Stained-glass leaded chandelier in Tiffany style, 1905-20

Above: Spring-powered pendulum clock, 1893
Below: Wall clock in walnut case, 1915

Three-piece ceramic syrup dispenser, 1895

Commemorative announcement with pocket-mirror inset

Watch fob, early 1900s

China plate, 1924

Trade card, issued by Western Coca-Cola Bottling Co., Chicago, 1900-1915. Caption: "Appearances are sometimes deceiving but Coca-Cola can always be relied on as nourishing, refreshing, and exhilarating."

Before it was discovered that thirst knows no season, Winter consumers were courted with Coca-Cola Chewing Gum, manufactured between 1908 and 1916.

"Export Bottle," used on luxury liners, 1927

The Western Coca-Cola Bottling Co. issued a series of Vienna art plates, lavishly framed and packed in velvet-lined boxes, 1905-1912.

Free-drink coupons were issued as early as 1886. These were printed between 1895 and 1905.

51

Coke for Different Folks

America's secret is its diversity within unity, a preservation of personal identity within a democracy's identification.

Perhaps the great secret is the knowledge of the components of the plural audience it seeks.

Enjoy the lively life of Coke

It's the real thing. Coke

It's the real thing.

Enjoy that REFRESHING NEW FEELING with Coca-Cola

Get that REFRESHING NEW FEELING with Coca-Cola

Be really refreshed! Bowl with Coke! Only Coca-Cola gives you the cheerful lift that's bright and lively... the cold crisp taste that deeply satisfies! No wonder Coke refreshes you best!

for THE PAUSE THAT REFRESHES

Harriet Tubman led 300 people to freedom.
She's one of America's great heroines.
Now there's an exciting new way to learn her story.

Coca-Cola

It's the real thing. Coke.

Real life calls for real taste.
For the taste of your life—Coca-Cola.
Here and now.

Pity the poor vending machine caught without Coke.
Alas, it may well be on its way to going broke.

It's the real thing. Coke.

It's the real thing. Coke

Real life calls for real taste.
For the taste of your life—Coca-Cola.
Here and now.

Give Me Your Tired, Your Hot, Your Thirsty...

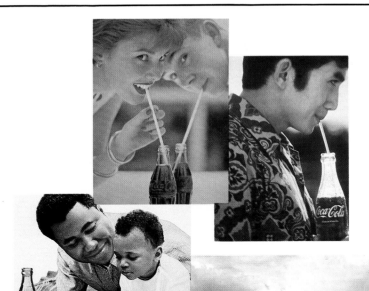

The year Coca-Cola was born—1886—coincided with the dedication of the Statue of Liberty, given by the people of France as a tribute to America's 100th birthday.

Liberty's inscription is ''The New Colossus,'' a sonnet by Emma Lazarus, whose lines include:

''Give me your tired, your poor,

''Your huddled masses yearning to breathe free,

''The wretched refuse of your teeming shore,

''Send these, the homeless, tempest-tossed to me:

''I lift my lamp beside the golden door.''

Lazarus' verse has inspired millions of Americans, immigrant and native-born alike.

It also inspired a stunning ad.

54

America,

Give me your tired, your hot, your thirsty, your weary, your parched, your worn-out, your mothers, your fathers, your sisters, your brothers, your sons, your daughters, your surfers, your skiers, your football players, your basketball players, your yachtsmen, your pole vaulters, your hockey stars, your lacrosse stars, your swimmers, your jockeys, your baseball players, your soccer players, your weight-lifters, your ping pong players, your chess enthusiasts, your checker whizzes, your bridge players, your poker players, your mah jong players, your kibitzers, your sun worshippers, your moon worshippers, your potato chip nuts, your pretzel eaters, your salted peanuts fans, your hot dog eaters, your hamburger eaters, your pizza pie eaters, your chili con carne devotees, your steelworkers, your scientists, your gefilte fish gourmets, your spaghetti eaters, your meat and potato men, your tuna fish eaters, your fried chicken experts, your bacon lettuce and tomato on toast eaters, your cabdrivers, your pilots, your stewardesses, your travel agents, your travelers, your poets, your construction men, your insurance salesmen, your diplomats, your secretaries, your telephone operators, your vacuum cleaner salesmen, your ushers, your hippies, your high school students yearning to pass math.

Things go better with Coke.

Trademarks, Signs and Symbols

In its soda-foundation infancy, Coca-Cola competed with half a hundred flavors. Within a few years it was coping with the first of what would become dozens of sound-alike imitations: Chero Cola, Cleo Cola, Coca & Cola, Coca-Lola, Coke-Ola, Co Kola, Kiko-Cola, Koko Kola, Ko-Kola, Kola Koke, Kola-Nola, Ola-Cola and Polo-Cola, to list only the most obvious ripoffs.

Slogans for Coke for 1913 included: "Ask for it by its full name—then you will get the genuine." Earlier ads had urged consumers to accept no substitutes, but since 1909 The Coca-Cola Company challenged the "Koke Co. of America" in a legal contest that was brought before the U.S. Supreme Court in 1920.

Associate Justice Oliver Wendell Holmes, delivering the Court's opinion, wrote:

"The name now characterizes a beverage to be had at almost any soda foundation.

"It means a single thing coming from a single source and well known to the community.

"In other words Coca-Cola probably means to most persons the plaintiff's familiar product to be had everywhere, rather than a compound of particular substances . . . ."

That didn't end The Coca-Cola Company's woes. Its lawyers have brought more than 400 suits in the 50-plus years since the Supreme Court ruling. The Coca-Cola Company's insistence on "the real thing" can be costly. The Coca-Cola Co. once spent some $100,000 to replace gallons of illicit Coke that dealers had unwittingly bought from an East Coast group counterfeiting Coke.

After the mid-Twenties, signs and advertisements avoided obscuring the famous trademark.

Tacky "Taka-Kola"

A judge's ruling in a 1921 suit brought by The Coca-Cola Co. against the makers of "Taka-Kola:"

"In the instant case the defendant's mark 'Taka-Kola' consists, as does 'Coca-Cola,' of two words, each of four letters and of two syllables. In each phrase a consonant and a vowel alternate, there being in each four of one and four of the other. . . The consonant 'l' is common to both . . . Plaintiff's contains three 'c's,' having in every instance the hard or 'k' sound. Twice defendant replaces the 'c' with a 'k,' and once by a 't,' the use of which last must be relied upon to distinguish the two words, for in every other respect they are for all practical purposes identical. The two words of plaintiff's are united by a hyphen; so are those of the defendant. The plaintiff displays its (mark) in script. The defendant has followed suit. . . . It taxes credulity to believe that so close a resemblance was accidental."

Missing Marks

The list of one-time trademarks that have entered the lower-case language includes these: aspirin, cellophane, corn flakes, cube steak, escalator, kerosene, lanolin, linoleum, milk of magnesia, mimeograph, mineral oil, nylon, phonograph, pocket book, shredded wheat.

Trademark Landmarks

1893—Trademark "Coca-Cola" registered in U.S. Patent Office.

1896—In its 10th year The Coca-Cola Company begins struggle with imitators.

1915—Root Glass Co., Terre Haute, Indiana, patents Alexander Samuelson's design for the classic bottle.

1920—U.S. Supreme Court rules that "Coke," when used for a beverage, means Coca-Cola and nothing else.

1929—Design for standard trademarked soda fountain glasses adopted.

1945—"Coke" registered as trademark.

1960—Design, contour and shape of THE bottle for Coke recognized as trademark by U.S. Patent Office.

Advertising Advice

The D'Arcy Advertising Agency masterminded ads for Coca-Cola from 1906 to 1956 when McCann-Erickson, Inc., which had handled The Coca-Cola Export Corporation's account in Latin America, was designated as the new advertising agency. The philosophy (keep it wholesome) remained unchanged.

In 1938 the D'Arcy Co. included the following suggestions in a 35-point list of guidelines:

+ Never split the trade mark "Coca-Cola" in two lines.

+ On oil paintings or color photographs be inclined to show a brunette rather than a blonde girl if only one girl is in the picture. Otherwise, show both.

+ In any illustration remember—adolescent girls or young women should be the wholesome type; not sophisticated-looking. Boys or young men should be wholesome, healthy types; not too handsome or sophisticated. Seldom show very old people, and never children under 6 or 7 years old.

+ Clothing, including hats, should be modern and up-to-date, but not extreme.

+ Never refer to Coca-Cola as "it."

+ Always say *"the pause that refreshes"* with ice-cold Coca-Cola"—never use it as synonymous with Coca-Cola.

+ Never make any exaggerated claim in copy beyond the fact that it is a delicious, refreshing, wholesome, pure drink—easily available.

In 1956, when McCann-Erickson took over the advertising account, seven "Conversational Guidelines about 'Coca-Cola' & 'Coke'" were issued for "the confidential use of radio announcers, disc jockeys and other program personnel." Among its directives:

+ Coca-Cola and its companion trademark, Coke, identify a particular brand of refreshment. These trademarks may be used any time you wish to talk about a situation in which something good to drink is appropriate, such as, "Man, wouldn't an ice-cold bottle of Coke go good right about now?"

(Never use Coca-Cola or Coke as a generic term . . .)

+ Like deer and elk and a host of other words, Coke and Coca-Cola are both singular and plural. Use each mark to represent one or many. The container (bottle, glasses or cups) Coke comes in may vary, but the trademark is always "Coke" or "Coca-Cola."

(Never say, "All the cats had Cokes." Instead, say, "All the cats had bottles—or glasses—of Coke"!)

+ Coca-Cola and Coke are of equal status trademark-wise and may be used interchangeably, but the trade-mark Coca-Cola must be used at least once in every commercial message.

(Never use Coke only, instead say Coke and then refer to the product as Coca-Cola the next time you mention the brand name.)

In a lengthy, 1968, eight-point brochure called *Philosophy of Coca-Cola Advertising,* "the market" was described:

+ It is a Mass Market. The first thing that occurs to us in considering our product is that it is obviously a mass one. That is, our product appeals to the entire population, without consideration for race, color or creed. We are interested in both sides of the railroad track. We are interested in both the salon and the saloon. We want to know Rosie O'Grady just as intimately as . . . the Colonel's Lady. . . .

+ The Market is a Parade. Each year, over a million people die in the United States. Contrary to our best efforts, this large group has been eliminated as consumers of our product. It is inevitable, therefore, that replacements must be found if our market is to be numerically maintained. Fortunately, there is a source of replacement. In 1967, 3,533,000 people were born in the United States. And many youngsters moved up into the Coca-Cola consuming age groups to replace those who had dropped off. The importance of these figures is not primarily to prove that we are living in an expanding economy, but to prove (what so many people overlook) that our market is a parade. It is never a static group to which we can address our remarks once and forget about advertising from then on. We cannot afford to stop putting coal in the engine once the train is in motion. Stop advertising and in a few short years, the cycle of death and birth will have produced a completely new set of customers no one of whom has ever heard of Coca-Cola. How many of these once famous household products do you now remember? Sapoleo, Sunny Jim, Fairy Soap, Pears Soap, the Gold Dust Twins?

Both trade-marks mean the same thing

The Artists of Coca-Cola

During the Twenties and Thirties, The Coca-Cola Company commissioned advertising art from top illustrators. The crop it harvested is still fresh.

N.C. Wyeth's fame as an illustrator of children's classics is shared rather than diminished by the work of his illustrious offspring—son Andrew and grandson Jamie.

John Newton Howitt's posters, like this one for 1923, were sunny, realistic scenes depicted with the lights and leaves of Impressionist masters.

Bradshaw Crandall's charming women were invariably refreshing in broad-brimmed hats almost as familiar as the more famous trademark.

Norman Rockwell's celebration of everyday Americana is evident in these calendars. His 1934 verandah scene could have been 1834 except for the Coke.

John Held Jr. caught the tempo of the Jazz Age in a sparse language of line.

An early Twenties ad series celebrated the solidity of small-town America through parades, train arrivals, fires. Names on storefronts and awnings include Fred Thompson, Art McCoy and William Doran, but no single painter of the sequence has been identified.

Held's Flappers and College-Boy Flaskers still epitomize an era more jagged than jazzy.

Frederic Stanley's The Village Blacksmith, *for the warm 1933 calendar, adds a dash of Coke to an American tradition then already passing into legend.*

Rockwell's farm boys with dogs sometimes were called "Tom Sawyer" and "Huckleberry Finn," but reflect Thirties realities more than Mark Twain fiction.

A Series to Savor

One of the most delectable series of ads appeared in publications geared to a somewhat limited audience (scholastic and racing-car publications).

Their wit laughs beyond limit.

We can't say for sure that a daily ration of Coca-Cola would have prevented the mutiny on the Bounty. But knowing, as we do, how the unique, refreshing taste of Coke lifts the spirits, we feel that an ice-cold bottle or two would certainly have put the men in a better frame of mind. What we don't understand is why Captain Bligh's immortal parting words, reproduced below in their entirety, were for some obscure reason left out of the history books.

A lot of people have the wrong idea about Marie Antoinette. She wasn't nearly so nasty as they say. For instance, when told that the peasants were starving and preparing to revolt, it occurred to her that the bright, clean, refreshing taste of Coca-Cola would lift their spirits and make things go a little better. So she suggested it, in the legendary words, "Let them drink Coke." Unfortunately, she was misquoted, and you know what happened after that. All of which goes to prove, we suppose, that you can't have your cake and drink it, too.

We're not exactly sure which historian it was who wrote, "Things would have gone better with Coke," in a widely ignored book about the active matrimonial career of Henry VIII. However, knowing as we do, how the big bold taste of Coca-Cola quenches even a king-sized thirst and restores the spirit, we can't help but agree that a frosty bottle or two, at the right moment, might have kept a number of people from losing their heads.

On the Ides of March, 44 BC, Julius Caesar, standing on the steps of the Senate, saw Brutus approaching. Assuming his friend would like a refreshing drink of ice-cold Coca-Cola, Caesar called out "Et tu Brute?" meaning, "You want some, too, Kiddo?" Unfortunately, Brutus had flunked Latin, and, thinking he'd been insulted, immediately slew Caesar, speaking the immortal words, "Res melius evinissent cum Coke," a translation of which appears below.

60

"Tout serait allé mieux avec Coke." Serious students of French history will recall these famous words (translated below) which were written in the sand of the Isle of Elba by the exiled Napoleon Bonaparte. Napoleon's fondness for the unique, bold taste of Coca-Cola (not to mention its refreshing lift) is well known, and is considered particularly significant in light of the fact that Coke wasn't invented for some 72 years after his exile.

"Things would have gone better with Coke."

"Tout serait alle mieux avec Coke." Serious students of French history will recall these famous words (translated below) which were written in the sand of the Isle of Elba by the exiled Napoleon Bonaparte. Napoleon's fondness for the unique, bold taste of Coca-Cola (not to mention its refreshing lift) is well known, and is considered particularly significant in light of the fact that Coke wasn't invented for some 72 years after his exile.

Anatomy of an Ad

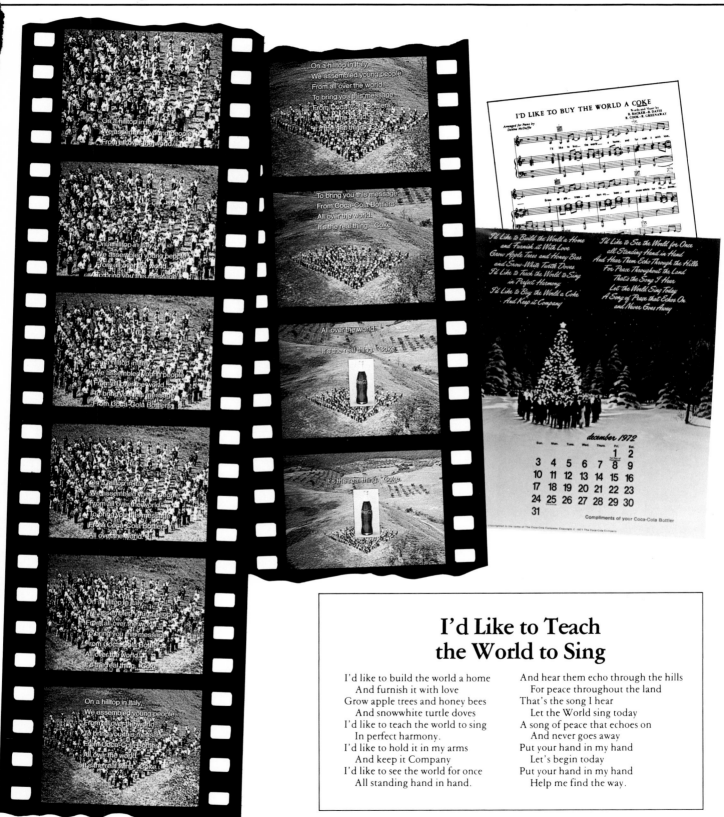

I'd Like to Teach the World to Sing

I'd like to build the world a home
  And furnish it with love
Grow apple trees and honey bees
  And snowwhite turtle doves
I'd like to teach the world to sing
  In perfect harmony.
I'd like to hold it in my arms
  And keep it Company
I'd like to see the world for once
  All standing hand in hand.

And hear them echo through the hills
  For peace throughout the land
That's the song I hear
  Let the World sing today
A song of peace that echoes on
  And never goes away
Put your hand in my hand
  Let's begin today
Put your hand in my hand
  Help me find the way.

Coke for the Presidents...

Vice President Harry Truman had just dropped into Speaker of the House Sam Rayburn's office for a bourbon highball when he heard the news from Warm Springs, Ga., in April, 1945, that President Roosevelt had died. Later, Truman, gassing up on the hustings, not only quenched his auto's thirst, but cooled his own with a bottle of Coke, a standard refreshment at gas stations.

President Dwight D. Eisenhower, who was graduated at 24 with an "A" in football from West Point (though he ranked 61st in his studies), received an ovation when he returned to Washington from Europe in June, 1945. The people liked him even more when he said, "I am neither a Republican nor a Democrat." He ranked high enough in 1952 to be elected President on the Republican ticket—and the Coke tasted as refreshing then as those he drank during World War II.

What went better during the years of "Camelot" than a bottle of Coke? President John F. Kennedy thought so, too, at a formal dinner during those years when the aura around the White House glowed with the same radiance that historians ascribed to the time of King Arthur.

President Lyndon Johnson's penchant for pulling beagles' ears to hear them yip may have cost him some votes, but he insisted the dogs liked it. Among the President's pleasures was "pressing the flesh" on the campaign trail, and between shaking the hands of countless well-wishers, he'd "pull" on something he also liked: a cool Coke.

Like all Presidents, Richard Nixon knew the turmoils and pressures of high office. But he also knew that a hamburger was the prelude to a special something that adds to life: a Coke.

and Castro, too.

64